GOD TELLS
THE SUN TO SHINE

Dear Punni'
with love
AB
Mar 15

GOD TELLS
THE SUN TO SHINE

An amazing story of love and forgiveness

Femi Bolaji

PARTRIDGE

A Penguin Random House Company

To order additional copies of this book, contact
Toll Free 0800 990 914 (South Africa)
+44 20 3014 3997 (outside South Africa)
orders.africa@partridgepublishing.com

www.partridgepublishing.com/africa

To
Kolawole Olaniyan Bolaji,
who taught me to read

And to the loving memory of
Rachael Funmilayo Bolaji,
who was by his side

Acknowledgments

My special thanks go to
Prof Ike Nwachukwu,
mentor, brother and friend, who
encouraged me to write this book

My thanks also go to
Philip John, April Ross, Syrah Mayell M. Denura,
Myradine S. Sedigo and the production team at Partridge

BEFORE SUNSET

There is a story in Genesis chapter 32 of the Bible. Jacob, the third in line of the patriarchs after Abraham and Isaac, wrestled with an angel on the bank of a brook called Jabbok. It beggars belief that a man would dare to wrestle with an angel of God. From other accounts, men and women were usually in awe if they so much as sighted one of those heavenly beings. So what gave this man the audacity that he had? What about the angel? Did he not have the powers to snuff out this impudent mortal in one fell swoop?

Jacob was a man for whom the birds had come home to roost, and the sins of his past had caught up with him. As a child, although he was the second-born of twin boys, he pined for the privileges that would come to his brother Esau, who was the firstborn. Esau was the heir apparent to their father, Isaac, and he would get double the inheritance that his siblings would get when Isaac died. Jacob, however, became so obsessed with his brother's privileges even when the boys were still in their teens. He began to plot how to take Esau's position.

Perhaps if Esau were to die young, Jacob thought, *then I will become the heir!*

But Esau was fit as a fiddle! The dude bristled with health from incidental workouts in the hunting fields around Beersheba in Canaan, where the family lived. Whenever Jacob saw their father, Isaac, knocking back an evening meal of meat skewers from Esau's hunting, his heart sank. God appeared to have put all the stars in only one man's sky!

Then Jacob thought, *Maybe I should kill him!*

He realised that attempting to kill his brother could go terribly wrong, so he did not dwell on the thought. He remembered a story their father, Isaac, had told them about two of their ancestors, Cain and Abel. They were brothers, but the younger one, Abel, was favoured by the God of the clan. Cain worked the soil while Abel kept flocks. In the course of time, Cain decided to make sacrifices to God. He knew from a story his own father, Adam, had told him that God preferred a sacrifice of unblemished animals, but Cain did not have any of his own.

Long before Cain and Abel were born, Adam and his wife, Eve, had sinned against God by deliberately disobeying him. But God loved them nonetheless, so He devised a way to stop Himself from constantly remembering their misdeed. God killed some lambs and covered the man and the woman with their skins. Thereafter whenever God looked at them, what He saw was the innocence of the lambs that were slain.

Although Cain knew God's preference, he was too proud to ask his brother for a lamb or two from Abel's own flock. Therefore, he offered some of the best of the fruits of his soil, but God did not accept this sacrifice.

Following in his brother's example, Abel also decided to sacrifice to God, but unlike his brother, he had paid attention to their father's story. He offered the fat of the firstborn of his flock. God sniffed at the burning sacrifice and loved it. But the more that God smiled, the more Cain's face fell. He feared that now that Abel had God's approval, he could easily become the alpha male. When Cain could no longer bear that thought, he lured Abel to an isolated field far from their settlement and killed him. God was so annoyed that He cursed Cain and drove him away.

Jacob did not want to make Cain's mistake. Therefore, he started to devise an alternative plan to upstage his brother.

Esau had a weakness—he lacked self-control. Often, after he returned from the fields, he would stop by at Jacob's pad to munch. When he was hungry, he was like a lion waiting impatiently to have a go at the kill. Jacob observed that the best time to get his brother to agree to about anything was while Esau was waiting for his food. Over time, Jacob hatched a plan to ask Esau to exchange his birthright for food on such a day that he was very hungry. At first, the idea appeared ludicrous, but as Jacob observed Esau, he realised that he had a winning plan.

Soon an opportunity came along. After a hunting trip on a fateful day, Esau returned home famished.

'Jacob!' he yelled. 'Quick, let me have some of that soup.'

But Jacob replied, 'Firstly, promise to trade places with me so that I will become the elder and you the younger brother.'

'What got into you?' Esau asked, puzzled at the request.

'Sorry, bruv,' Jacob parried, 'no deal, no dine.'

Esau walked away towards their mother's tent, bemused. He reckoned that Rebekah would have some leftovers from lunch, but she was not in. *Mum would have gone to water her vegetable garden*, Esau thought. He nosed around the kitchen; the fireplace was cold. As he returned, the smell of Jacob's cooking wafted to his nostrils in the cool evening air. "Boy, I'm starving!" he thought out loud. He returned to his brother, thinking, *Can Jacob really become the firstborn simply by sharing his food with me? He is out of his mind. Whoever heard of such a thing?* Esau decided to play along, thinking that he would get the soup for nothing, but Jacob was eagerly awaiting his brother's return.

'Deal?' Jacob asked when he sighted Esau.

'What use is the birthright to me if I die of hunger?' Esau muttered.

'Swear to me,' Jacob pressed him.

Esau was getting angry, but there did not seem to be a way around Jacob's insistence. It occurred to him that since nobody had witnessed their conversation, he could say afterwards say that he did not really mean to trade places with his brother. At any rate, he was sure that their father, Isaac, would not recognise such an exchange.

'I swear,' Esau replied.

Jacob served his brother some bread and soup. Esau was bewildered at how resolute Jacob appeared, but he shrugged off an alarm bell that started to go off in his head. He ate and drank, and then he got up and left.

Fait accompli! Jacob was elated. Afterwards, when their mother returned, he told her about the transaction that evening with Esau, but he had not anticipated her reaction. Rebekah drew her breath sharply and beat her breasts. She had not imagined that Jacob could do such a thing.

'It was wrong of you to have done that!' she scolded him.

Jacob was embarrassed.

'Have you mentioned it to your father?' Rebekah probed further.

'No,' he replied, shaking his head.

'Let this be the last anyone would hear of it,' she warned him sternly.

Jacob nodded as he slunk off. He felt like a child caught with his hand in the cookie jar.

The happenings that day would, however, change the course of Jacob's life and the destiny of the entire race. All that he wanted was to be the head of the family when their father died. He despised his brother and felt that he possessed better qualities than Esau, thus making him more eligible to be the leader of the pack. After all, Esau was only older than him by a few moments.

But why was Jacob so engrossed in this desire for his brother's place?

SCHEMING AND CONNIVING

When Rebekah was pregnant, she had such a particularly hard time, and many times she felt there was a struggle going on inside her. It was her first pregnancy after a delay of about twenty years that she married her husband, Isaac. When she should have been glowing with pride at her blossoming baby bump, she was so distraught that she cried out in anguish, 'Why am I like this?'

So she went to a seer, who told her, 'There are two people in your womb who are butting heads before they are born. One shall be stronger than the other, and the older shall serve the younger.'

God's answer offered her little comfort and confused her further, so she hung on for dear life for the rest of her term. At delivery, Esau was the first to come out, followed closely by his brother Jacob. When he came out, Jacob clutched tightly to his twin brother's heel with his fist such that the midwife called out 'You cheat!' as she separated them.

As the boys grew, Isaac, their father, loved Esau, but Rebekah loved Jacob. Isaac's affirmation of Esau, however, was not only because he was the heir apparent. Rather, the man loved gamey meats, and Esau ensured copious supplies from his hunting. Isaac thus did not acknowledge his younger son or reassure him of his fatherly affection. He was not a bad father, but he failed to recognise the peculiar challenge that twins face while developing their individual identities. Jacob was therefore left to his mother, who provided the nurturing and recognition that his young soul needed.

Rebekah loved Jacob. He was like the daughter she would never have. The boy loved to stay at home and keep her company, so she had the opportunity to teach him invaluable life skills, like tenacity and delayed gratification. Jacob, however, grew to be highly competitive, needing his father's attention as much as his elder brother. He smouldered at the privileges reserved for his twin brother, who was being groomed to be the head of the family.

Although they were a small monogamous family, the parents unwittingly set the stage for much of the rivalry between their children by playing favourites so openly. Jacob, being the younger son, was particularly affected and suffered from feelings of insecurity and low self-esteem. He was unable to come to terms with their father's apparent preferential treatment of Esau.

In the course of time, Isaac grew old, and his thoughts went to passing the baton of leadership to his firstborn son, Esau. By this time, Isaac could hardly see, but he had not lost his appetite for game. His happiest moments were when he was sampling meats with his few remaining teeth in the cool evening shade, his eyes glistening with tears as he relieved countless stories of his life's sojourn.

Isaac sent for Esau and instructed him, 'Go out hunting and prepare a meal for me from your kill.'

'Yes, Dad,' Esau replied, surprised. Isaac had been poorly for some days and unable to eat. His breakfast was still in the corner of his tent, untouched.

'But, Dad,' he continued, 'you haven't touched your breakfast. Do you have the appetite?'

'Do as I say, son, I am an old man now and near to the grave. I must bless you as my father blessed me before I die. I would like to eat of your hunt one more time.'

Esau was uncomfortable with his father's talk of dying. But when Isaac saw that his son hesitated, he prodded him on, 'Go on, son, and don't be long.'

As Esau left the tent, he almost ran into Rebekah, who was standing at the door. He wondered for how long she had been there and whether she had overheard the conversation with Isaac.

'Hello, Mum,' he greeted, rushing off.

'Hello, Esau,' Rebekah replied. She had gone to see how her husband was doing when she heard voices coming from his tent. Esau had drawn close to his father's bed in order to hear the old man's slurred speech, and so he had not noticed that his mother stood nearby and could hear their conversation. It was painful for Rebekah to see her dear husband's strength ebb away. The twenty-five-odd years between them meant that as Isaac grew older, his wife became his caregiver, and it was a role she carried out meticulously.

Rebekah was horrified at what she heard, and she felt the blood drain from her face. She knew that this day would come, and she mulled over her life after Isaac was gone. She worried endlessly over thoughts of the family fortunes and responsibilities passing on to her firstborn son. Esau was a wild one who, to mark his fortieth birthday, had married two local girls—Judith and Basemath. They were uncouth and were constantly fighting each other in a hitherto peaceful household. They brought grief to their aged parents-in-law.

Rebekah often thought about God's reply to her inquiry many years ago during her difficult pregnancy with her twins. At the time, God had said, 'The older of the boys shall serve the younger.' She also remembered a story Jacob had once related to her, how he had manipulated Esau to exchange the position of the firstborn son with him. She had long judged that Jacob would make a better leader of the family than Esau, so she decided on the spot to thwart Isaac's plan to anoint their first son.

Soon after Esau left to go hunting, Rebekah found Jacob and, pulling him into her tent, commanded him breathlessly, 'Come here quickly! Your father has just asked Esau to prepare a meal for him. He wants to give him God's blessing and to anoint him as the leader of the family. Now, do what I tell you. Go and get two young goats, kill them, and I will prepare a meal like your father loves. Then you will take it to him so that he can bless you instead.'

It was the moment that Jacob had longed for, but he hesitated at the audacity of Rebekah's plan.

'But, Mum,' Jacob began, 'Esau is hairy, and I have smooth skin. What if Dad feels me? He'll curse me instead.'

Rebekah replied, 'If that happens, I'll take the curse on myself. Just do what I say.'

Jacob didn't need much persuasion. The situation was urgent, and he had learned to trust his mother's judgement. His heart pounding, he went and brought the meat to Rebekah, and she prepared a delicacy for Isaac. She also gave Jacob one of Esau's coats which he had left in her tent, then she asked him to cover his hands and the nape of his neck with goatskins.

'Take it to your father and sit with him while he eats,' Rebekah instructed Jacob.

When Jacob got to Isaac's tent, the old man, thinking it was Esau, was surprised that he had returned so quickly.

'How did you get it so quickly?' Isaac asked.

'Your God brought it to me,' Jacob replied.

Isaac asked his son to come closer so that he could feel him.

'The voice is Jacob's, but the hands are Esau's. Are you sure you are really Esau, my son?'

'Yes, I am,' Jacob answered quickly, pale as death.

Isaac hesitated in a pensive mood; he worried whether it was really Esau his firstborn son. Afterwards, he shrugged his frail shoulders and then fell to, enjoying the meal as at other times. Jacob also brought some wine, and his father drank, then Isaac blessed Jacob, placing his right hand on his head.

> May God give you of Heaven's dew
> And Earth's bounty of grain and wine
> May peoples serve you and nations honour you
> You will master your brothers
> And your mother's sons will honour you
> Those who curse you will be cursed
> And those who bless you will be blessed.
> (Genesis 27:28–29) MSG

Immediately after his father had blessed him, Jacob hurriedly cleared the wooden dishes and dashed out. He went to find Rebekah, who was waiting anxiously in her tent, her heart in her mouth. When she saw Jacob, she sprang up from her bed; her eyes searched his face. Jacob nodded nervously.

'Dad b-b-blessed me!' he stuttered.

They spoke quietly as if they feared that the tents would hear their hushed secret. Rebekah then knelt and bowed her head to God in worship. When she arose, she shushed her son out of the tent, indicating with her hands that he should go away from the compound quickly. He understood her gestures; the bond between mother and child was such that Rebekah did not have to say a word for Jacob to know her mind.

Not long afterwards, Esau returned and prepared for his father a platter of well-done meats from his hunting.

'Sit up, Dad, I've brought your meal,' he called out.

'And who are you?' Isaac asked, bemused.

'Esau.'

'But I had already eaten your food and blessed you.' Isaac struggled to sit up, bewildered at the unfolding drama.

'No, Dad, I have just returned from the hunt.'

Isaac was shaken! He leaned back in his bed and supported his grey head in his right hand as if that would help to focus his thinking.

'Your brother came here and took your blessing by deceit!' He sighed weakly.

'Ha!' Esau wailed. Immediately, he remembered that afternoon many years ago when Jacob had asked that they exchange birth positions. Although he had not forgotten the incident, he did not imagine that it would ever come to this.

'Don't you have a blessing for me, Dad?'

'I have made him your master, and that will surely be,' Isaac explained.

Esau lay on the dung-coated floor, sobbing. When Isaac saw that his son was inconsolable, pleading, 'Bless me, Dad, please bless me,' he motioned for him to draw close, then he placed his left hand on Esau's head and said:

> You'll live far from Earth's bounty
> Remote from Heaven's dew
> You'll live by your sword
> From hand-to-mouth
> And you'll serve your brother
> But when you can't take it any more
> You'll break loose and run free.
> (Genesis 27:39–40) MSG

Esau was overwhelmed with regret. He realised how frivolous he had been to have fallen for Jacob's scheming many years ago. He seethed with anger as he left his father's tent to go and look for Jacob, but the scoundrel was nowhere to be found. Then he went to Rebekah's tent to report the matter to her, but she was not in either. He went and stood at the entrance to the compound, looking up and down at the dirt road to see if Jacob would appear. However, the trickster stayed away from home for a couple of days until the rush of Esau's wrath subsided.

Over the next few days, Rebekah talked things over with Isaac until he was comforted and forgave his younger son for the deception. They had shared a good life together and agreed on most things except in the matter of the upbringing of their children.

However, Esau had resolved that if he could not have the blessing, neither would Jacob. So he made up his mind to kill him. He would, however, wait until after Isaac's death so as not to hasten his father's demise. He reckoned that he would not have to wait very long as Isaac was already at death's door.

When Rebekah heard that Esau was plotting to kill his brother, she took the matter to Isaac, and they agreed that it would be better for Jacob to keep away from Beersheba for a while. Together, they decided to send him to Rebekah's family in Harran. They reasoned it would also afford Jacob an opportunity to find a well-brought-up girl from his mother's family as his wife.

On that same day, Isaac sent for Jacob and told him of their plans to send him away to Paddan Aram in the country of Harran, which was 500 miles away from Beersheba. He would go and live with his uncle Laban, who was Rebekah's brother. Jacob knelt before both his parents while Isaac confirmed upon him once again the family blessing.

Jacob realised that there was no way out but to flee from Beersheba in order to escape Esau's indignation. The urgency required was such that he did not even have the time to put his house in order; he left without taking anything with him save for the clothes on his back and his staff.

STARTING ALL OVER

Just before dawn the following day, Jacob left Beersheba to travel to Harran on foot. By sunset, he arrived at a city called Luz, and he decided to camp there. It was the first day of his journey, and he was dog-eared tired. He curled up under the open skies and used a stone for a pillow. That night, he had a strange dream. He saw himself kneeling in prayer at the foot of a ladder with its top reaching to the sky. As he prayed, fearsome-looking angels went up the ladder as if bearing his prayers and afterwards returned down the ladder towards him.

Then God himself appeared and said to him, 'I am the God of Abraham and Isaac, your fathers. I will give this very ground on which you are sleeping to you and your children. You will become a race stretching from west to east and from north to south. I will be with you on this journey and bring you back here.'

As soon as God had finished speaking, Jacob awoke with a start. In the first few moments, he was unsure where he was. Then his memory rushed back, and he recollected how he had stolen away from Beersheba the previous day. He scrambled to his feet, his clothes wet from the early-morning dew. He was puzzled at the meaning of his dream.

Does God not care that I obtained my father's blessing fraudulently? he pondered. Then it dawned on him that God had just given him the thumbs up as the progenitor of the race! Jacob was elated! He decided that the city would be renamed Bethel, meaning 'House of God', when God fulfilled His promise and gave it to him.

He also made a vow in his heart to God: 'If you will stand by me, protect me, provide for me, and bring me back to Canaan in one piece, then you will be my God. I will also give to you a tenth of everything that you give me.'

At daybreak, when Jacob resumed on his journey towards Canaan, there was a hint of a swagger in his stride. The encounter with God in his dream had been so reassuring.

He thought to himself, *Surely, the stay at Harran would only be for a short while before I can return to my father's house.* It seemed to him that the end justified the means after all.

However, unknown to Jacob, he was to spend over twenty years in exile before he could ever return to Beersheba, and the shadows which had been cast over him by the setting sun on that first evening of his flight when he had arrived at Luz would not lift as quickly as he had anticipated.

After what appeared to him to be an unending journey, Jacob finally arrived at a grazing field on the outskirts of

Paddan Aram. He saw a well with several herds of animals bedded around it. The well was covered with a huge stone, so the shepherds would wait for one another before pulling together to roll the stone away from the well and giving water to their animals.

'Hey, guys,' Jacob called out to some of the men who were there with the flocks. 'Where are you from?'

They answered him, 'We're from Harran.'

Jacob was excited, and he asked hurriedly, 'Do you know Laban, Nahor's son? Is he well?'

'Yeah,' they replied. 'Here comes his daughter Rachel with her father's flock.'

Jacob froze! His heart fluttered as he observed Rachel confidently round up her herd. The young girl was stunning and was unlike anyone he had ever set his eyes on.

Quickly he walked up to her and offered to roll the stone away from the well and also to help to water her sheep.

'We have to wait for the other shepherds to arrive,' Rachel protested.

'Not to worry,' said Jacob. Before she could say another word, Jacob had single-handedly rolled the stone away and drawn enough water for the sheep. He ran back and forth from the well to the watering trough where the animals huddled together to drink.

Rachel observed the agile stranger, bemused.

'Why are you doing this?' she asked.

Jacob broke into tears as he related to Rachel that they were cousins and that he had just arrived from Canaan, which was 500 miles away, to find her family.

On hearing this, Rachel ran and told her father, Laban, excitedly, 'Aunty Rebekah's son is here from Canaan!'

Together, father and daughter ran back to the well, where Jacob had stayed with the sheep. Laban was very happy to see his sister's son for the very first time and welcomed Jacob warmly. Then they returned home to the rest of the family. In the evening, they all gathered to eat at the family square, and Jacob filled them in with stories about his parents and life in Canaan. He was careful not to mention the rift with his brother Esau. Rather, he told Laban that his mother was anxious to re-establish contact with her family again and so had sent him away to Harran to find them. Laban welcomed him to stay with his family for as long as he wished. So Jacob settled in and went out with his cousins and Laban's servants daily to care for the flocks.

After Jacob had been at Harran for one month, Laban, wanting to formalise work arrangements with the new arrival, asked Jacob to name his wages to work on the pastures, whereupon the maverick jumped in. 'I will serve you seven years for Rachel, your younger daughter.'

Laban was gobsmacked at Jacob's proposition. He had not even begun to think about Rachel's betrothal and eventual marriage.

'Well,' he parried, 'I guess that it is better that I should give her to you than to another man. Remain with us, and we shall see.'

Rachel was the younger daughter, and it was against their custom for her to marry before her elder sister, Leah. Laban therefore hoped that God would send a deserving suitor to Leah before he would have to give Rachel's hand out in marriage. Meanwhile, Jacob kept his pledge faithfully, tending Laban's flocks for seven years, and the years passed quickly because he loved Rachel dearly.

At the end of seven years, Jacob expected that Laban would ask him to begin to prepare for his impending wedding to Rachel, but Laban did not. Jacob, therefore, looked out for an opportunity when his uncle was alone and in a good mood before broaching the subject with him.

'May God bless you, my father,' Jacob started. 'It is now seven years after I promised to serve you for Rachel's hand in marriage. At that time, I did not have the bride price, or I would have paid it. I have served you faithfully as promised. Please give Rachel to me to be my wife.'

Jacob had learned to approach Laban cautiously. The older man was impulsive. If Laban said 'Fat chance!' that was the end of the matter in spite of the agreements between the two men! Laban was quiet for a while as though he needed to think about Jacob's request. Finally he said, 'I will call for a meeting of the men to talk about the matter tomorrow.'

There was something about Laban's tone of voice and the look on his face that made Jacob apprehensive. He did not sleep much and feared that something was amiss.

A HUSBAND OF MANY

The following day, Laban called for a meeting of the men as he had promised, and they spent quite some time in deliberation. Afterwards, he sent for Jacob and told him that his wedding to Rachel had been agreed. Jacob was overjoyed as he fell at Laban's feet, thanking him.

The wedding was elaborate and lasted a whole week. On the last day, Laban made a feast for the entire community. The bride was finely attired and was attended by maidens. She wore a veil all through, but Jacob was not called upon to lift the veil as was the custom. In his excitement, he did not think much about it; rather, he wished that his family could have been at his wedding. He was sure that his mother would love Rachel, his bride; the boy had done good!

That night after all the wedding guests had departed, the newly-weds retired to their new home and their first night together. Bliss at last! In the morning, however, there was pandemonium at Casa Jacob. The groom was horrified to find out that instead of his beloved Rachel, he had been given her elder sister, Leah. Jacob was confused. He rubbed his eyes hard to make sure that he was not having a bad dream; afterwards, he became properly vexed.

'Seven years!' he cried out in anguish, clasping his head between his hands.

Because he had been with Leah the previous night, he knew from the customs of the tribe that there was now no way out of marrying her. Leah would not answer any of Jacob's angry questions; rather, she started to sob gently, feeling very embarrassed. The friends of the bridegroom who had slept overnight in the adjoining tents heard Jacob's angry cries, so they rushed in to investigate. Everyone was shocked! They helped Jacob to get dressed, and they all headed to Laban's house for an explanation. They found Laban seated with the men of the family at the entrance to his tent as though he was expecting to see Jacob.

'What have you done to me?' Jacob blurted out. 'I worked all those years for Rachel, why had you deceived me?'

Laban did not offer any explanations until everyone was seated. Then he cleared his throat and simply stated in a matter-of-fact tone of voice, 'Jacob, as you well know, we cannot give a girl away while she has an older sister who is yet to be married. We therefore decided to give Leah to you instead. If you still want Rachel, enjoy your honeymoon week with Leah, after which I will give Rachel to you also. However, it will cost you another seven years of your labour!'

Jacob was stunned! Words failed him, and he stuttered incoherently each time he tried to respond to Laban's weird proposition. Finally, his friends led him home. He spent the night alone and was very confused. From what he remembered of the constant fighting between Esau's two wives back at Beersheba, he did not want two women in his life. He considered letting go of Rachel and sticking with Leah, but the problem was that he did not love Leah! Besides, he could not bear the thought of his Rachel being with another man.

He longed for his mother, Rebekah, who used to be his confidant. She would know what to do in a situation such as this. The only way he could have Rachel was by slaving away for another seven-year period for Laban. The man surely had him in a corner. Would he be able to provide for his growing household as a farmhand?

Those were the thoughts that plagued his mind that night before he fell into a fitful sleep. He had a dream of Rachel; she was drawing water at the communal well for the camels of a man whose face he was unable to make out in his dream. When she finished, she placed her left hand in the strange man's right hand, and together they walked away towards Laban's tent. It was such a bad omen, and Jacob awoke with a start. Afterwards, he could not get back to sleep, so he sat up on his straw bed and leaned against the wall in his misery.

His thoughts went to Esau and how he had cheated his brother of his birthright. He wondered whether he was being justly punished for the sins of his youth. After all, what goes round comes round, they say, and a person reaps what they have sown. How could he expect to reap a harvest of virtue having sown seeds of discord? He often thought about life in Canaan, his parents, and his only brother. He reasoned that if he only was able to retrace his steps, he would not try as hard to usurp Esau's position. Back home, he was celebrated as the second in line to the family wealth, their father being a man of means.

At Paddan Aram, he was a mere hireling, toiling under the elements in order to earn his keep and to pay the price for his intended bride from the sweat of his brow. It also weighed him down that Laban was a taskmaster who did not accord his nephew any privileges but dealt shrewdly with him like any other farmhand. Jacob had somewhat mellowed over the years, and he sometimes wondered if the adventure to Harran had been worthwhile.

By the end of the week, Jacob realised that he had no choice but to agree to Laban's offer, so he set out to prepare a tent for Rachel. Leah and her maid Zilpah had moved into the one he had prepared for Rachel. Leah was as much a victim of circumstance as were Jacob and Rachel. The local matchmaker had tried but had not been able to find her an eligible suitor.

Laban therefore hatched a plan to marry off both his daughters to Jacob and thereby taking out two birds with one stone. That way, he would also get seven more years of Jacob's labour. He liked Jacob for his work ethic and did not mind having him as a son-in-law. Laban was sure his daughters would be well looked after, but he worried that Jacob would want to return to his country, Canaan, at some point in the future.

He remembered vividly that day, fifty years before, when his sister Rebekah, Jacob's mum, had left Harran to go to Canaan with a messenger who had come from over there to seek her hand in marriage to his master's son, Isaac. That was the last time that Laban had seen Rebekah. He doted over his daughters and would miss them terribly when the time came for them to fly the nest to build their own.

'Such is the way of life.' Laban sighed. If Jacob agreed to serve him for another seven-year period, he could keep his entire family together for longer.

After the honeymoon week, Rachel and her maid, Bilhah, moved in with Jacob and Leah at their new home. In spite of their circumstances, Jacob was delighted that he now had Rachel, and so he loved her more than her sister, Leah. The women therefore started an unprecedented rivalry for their husband's affection that soon turned the newly formed homestead into a beehive of dysfunction.

While Rachel was unable to have children, Leah had four boys in a row—Reuben, Simeon, Levi, and Judah! The names she gave to her sons showed her sense of triumph over her rival. In desperation, Rachel gave her maid, Bilhah, to her husband as a surrogate mother for a child. Jacob agreed, wanting to please his wife. The maid had two sons, and Rachel named them Dan and Naphtali.

This prompted Leah to give her own maid, Zilpa, to Jacob as well. Again, he consented in order to be fair. Zilpah had two sons—Gad and Asher. Then Leah resumed having children and gave birth to two boys—Issachar and Zebulun—and the family's only daughter, Dinah. By this time, Rachel was sorely wounded, and so she cried out to God in anguish for her own child. And God answered Rachel. She became pregnant and gave birth to a son, whom she called Joseph, meaning 'God will yet add to me'.

So Jacob had four women, ten sons, and a daughter in his life. For a man who had laboured for fourteen years so he could eventually have the woman he loved, his life was far from simple as he settled unending domestic squabbles between the women and their children.

IT TAKES ONE TO KNOW ONE

It was not long after Jacob started working for Laban that he observed that the older man was not to be taken at his word. However, he had no warning of Laban's grand scheme to deceive him into marrying Leah instead of Rachel. Although Jacob himself was a shifty sort of guy, he met more than a match in Laban.

After working for the contracted fourteen-year period and thereby earning the keep of his two wives, Jacob decided that it was time to return to his own country with his family and belongings. He was now in his sixties and was the head of a small tribe, including his two wives, two concubines, ten sons and a daughter, and many servants. He thought about it for a while before he ventured to ask his father-in-law.

'I want to return to my country with my wives and children for whom I have served you.'

Laban had seen this coming, so he had an answer ready for the younger man. 'Please stay here with me, my son.

You know that God has blessed me in the time that you have been here. Now that you have finished paying for your wives, name your price to be a manager in the business.'

Jacob was wary of Laban's offer. 'Please let me go, it is time for me to do something for my family. I have served you well, and your flocks have done well in my care.'

But Laban would not give in so easily. 'Please stay,' he pleaded. 'I will pay you well.'

Jacob realised that his father-in-law would not release him willingly, but he did not feel comfortable about continuing to work for Laban either. At the end, he came up with a business plan, which he laid out before Laban.

'You should not have to pay me. For my wages, please separate all the cattle and goats that are speckled or spotted and all the brown ones among the sheep. These will be mine, but the plain-coloured ones will be yours, and I will continue to care for your flocks.'

Jacob reasoned that this would help to clearly mark out which of the animals were his from the ones that belonged to Laban. Laban, likewise, felt that it was a fair deal as a majority of the animals were of one colour. He separated Jacob's share, and for good measure, he added the streaked male goats and put them all under the charge of his own sons at a distance of about fifty miles away from Jacob. He was confident that one-coloured animals would only produce one-coloured offspring, and therefore, his own share of the flocks would increase. So Jacob continued to look after Laban's flock.

In the mating season, Jacob had a dream wherein God's angel directed him to mate white female sheep and goats with striped, speckled, and spotted males. He, however, had only plain-coloured flocks in his care as Laban had since separated the speckled and spotted ones. Jacob thought long and hard and devised a plan to tamper with nature and make Laban's one-coloured sheep and goats produce striped, spotted, and specked offspring.

He took fresh shoots from poplar, almond, and sycamore trees and peeled white streaks in them, and these he placed beside watering troughs where Laban's flocks drank. Jacob's plan worked. By a strange coincidence, when plain-coloured white and black flocks which had been so exposed to the streaked rods mated, they produced striped, speckled, or spotted offspring. Jacob quickly separated them and added them to his own flocks.

Jacob, who had not quite forgiven Laban for deceiving him into marrying Leah several years earlier, saw an opportunity to get even. He only mated the stronger animals this way, but the weaker ones he left to breed naturally. That way, he soon owned more of the flocks and became more prosperous than his father-in-law. Laban and his sons thus started to grumble about Jacob's growing affluence, and their attitude towards him changed such that he feared that they would hurt him.

Then God appeared to Jacob and said, 'Return to Canaan, your country, and I will be with you.'

THE FLIGHT

Cyprian Ekwensi in *Burning Grass* describes a character's struggle in sub-Saharan Africa with a wandering disease he called sokugo. It results from a curse and strikes without warning. Sokugo compels men to wander off from all that they have toiled for at a time that they should be settling in. It thus deprives them of a stable life through having to start over and over again. Could it be the case that Jacob was likewise afflicted with such a disease?

Twenty years earlier, he had fled the security of his country to Harran, where mercifully he found respite with Laban, his uncle. Now he was on the run back to Canaan! At both times, it was a result of the dubious streak in his character that he was forced to flee. When he was at Canaan, he had deceived his father and robbed his brother of an inheritance to which he was not entitled but which he desperately desired. Afterwards, at Harran, he cast covetous eyes at his uncle's flocks, and he manipulated his way until he had dispossessed the old man of his life's work. Jacob was industrious, and God's hand was upon him, enabling him to prosper wherever he went, but time and again, the flaw in his character prevented him from finishing well.

It is remarkable though that at those times, when Jacob was running away from facing the consequences of his misdeeds, God would appear to him to encourage and reassure him. What did God see in this bent fellow that He was thus fascinated with him (more so God is presented in the good book as loving justice and hating wrongdoing)?

Despite his failings, it would appear that Jacob recognised that God was a promise-keeper and so could not break His covenant with his forebears. Jacob therefore keyed into that. The birthright which his brother Esau despised did not only convey privileges, it entailed responsibilities— you can't have the one and not the other.

Esau wanted the privileges, but Jacob embraced the responsibilities. An essential part of the responsibilities was the perpetuity of the race through offspring to be born of God-inspired marriage relationships, for God had promised their grandfather Abraham in his old age when he did not have a child: 'I will make you exceedingly fruitful. I will make nations of you, and kings shall come from you.'

On the night that Jacob spent at Luz after he had escaped from being killed by Esau, God had appeared to him in a dream. Afterwards, Jacob built an altar to God as a memorial to His promise to preserve him, saying, 'If You will keep me, feed and clothe me, and bring me back to my father's house, then You will be my God, and I will give You a tenth of all that You give me.' Twenty years down the line, when he faced certain death at the prospect of meeting his brother Esau again, Jacob would remind God about that promise. Jacob was a spiritual man after all, and God therefore could not ignore him.

Once Jacob had decided to flee from Harran, he consulted his wives to test the waters if they would go with him. He sent for them to meet him at the fields where he was tending the flock.

When they arrived he said to them, 'Rachel and Leah, I have noticed that your father has changed towards me. He no longer treats me as well as he did before. You know how hard I have worked for him, but he has cheated me time and again, but God has not let him hurt me until now. He's very angry with me now because my flocks have greatly increased over his. Yet it was my God who taught me how to manage the flocks, and He has now instructed me in a dream to get out of here and return to Canaan.'

Rachel was the first to speak up. Her feelings of resentment towards her father ran deep. She had not forgiven him for marrying off her elder sister, Leah, in her place to her beloved Jacob many years earlier. She believed that her father was more interested in the bride price and so had treated them both as chattels. If only Laban had asked her opinion, she would gladly have waited for Leah to find her own man rather than end up sharing her man with three other women.

Leah felt the same way about their father. The constant bickering over the years with the other women and their children had worn her down. She also believed that Laban should have given her more time for the matchmaker to find her a suitable man. For once, the women were uncharacteristically united in their answer to their husband.

'Our father has not treated us well by pitting us against each other as rivals. All he wanted was the bride price. Whatever you have now belongs to us and our children. We will go with you wherever your God directs you.'

Having gained his wives' consent, Jacob prepared to escape from Harran with his family and all his belongings. He concealed the plan so well from Laban that he made away with everyone and everything that he owned. It also helped that Laban had assigned him to distant fields on the outskirts of town where he reared the flocks. He soon crossed the Euphrates River and headed for the Gilead mountain ranges.

It was three days before Laban heard the news. 'Jacob has escaped!' Quickly he set up a search party of his sons and servants, and they chased after the runaways. After seven days of hard driving, Laban caught up with them at Gilead, where they had stopped to rest.

However, prior to the encounter, God had appeared to Laban in a dream, warning, 'Be careful what you do to Jacob.' The strange dream bothered Laban; his intention had been to take back the women with their children and flocks and to send Jacob away empty-handed. He, thus, pondered on what to do as he approached them.

Laban was livid when he eventually caught up with Jacob. 'Why did you run off with my daughters and grandchildren like a thief in the night? Did you think I would not hear of it and catch up with you? I would destroy you now if not for the God of your father who appeared to me last night and said not to hurt you. You did not only take my flocks, you also stole my household idols!'

Jacob knew that the odds were stacked against him, so he chose his words carefully. 'I was scared, sir, that you would take your daughters away from me. But I didn't take your teraphim.'

Jacob did not know that Rachel had taken the idols. She felt vindictive towards her father and was happy at the chance to hurt him. She had taken the idols to prevent Laban from using them in divination and enquiring of their whereabouts; besides, the teraphim were valuable if she could sell them.

Jacob was so sure that no one had the idols that he cursed, 'If you find the idols with anyone of us, that person will die.'

Rachel therefore feared being found out that she put the idols in a camel cushion and sat on them. When the searchers came into her tent, she excused herself for not getting up. 'Dad, don't think that I am being disrespectful by not getting up, it is my time of the month.'

Shamefaced, Laban retreated from searching the tents, and it was Jacob's turn to be angry.

'Are you satisfied now that I would never steal from you? In the twenty years that I slaved away for you—fourteen years for your daughters and six years looking after your flock—you made me pay if anything happened to your flocks, whether they miscarried or were taken by wild animals. Ten times you changed my pay, and if the God of my father had not been on my side, you would have sent me away penniless.'

Laban defended himself. 'Everything is mine—the women, the children, and flocks.' He realised that the time had come, which he had dreaded, to let go of Jacob with his wives and children. It was also obvious that they were all happy to be with their husband and father.

As was their tradition of settling boundary disputes, the men set up a monument of stones, and Laban swore over them, 'From now on, these stones will be a witness between you and me when you are out of my sight. If you mistreat my daughters or take other wives after them, God will see you and judge you. I will not cross this line to hurt you, and you must not cross to hurt me either.'

'So shall it be,' Jacob pledged.

Afterwards, they all sat down to eat a meal, and they slept that night on Mount Gilead. The following morning, Laban rose early; he kissed his daughters and grandchildren and blessed them. As he returned home, he wept at the pain of separation from the ones he loved.

THE FIGHT

After Laban and his group had left, Jacob braced himself for what he felt would be the mother of all battles of his life to date—the encounter with his brother Esau. He had not told his wives the details of what had actually happened twenty years earlier between Esau and himself. If the women knew, they would have realised that staying back at Harran with their father was a lesser evil than fleeing to Canaan. When Jacob was alone ruminating about his dilemma, suddenly he saw some angels. He had come to realise that each time an angel appeared to him, it was either to encourage him or to guide him. This time the angels told him how he was to prepare to meet with his brother Esau.

Jacob found some local people and paid them to run an errand to his brother Esau at Seir. He instructed them according to the guidance the angels gave them.

'Say to Esau: "Your servant Jacob, who has been living in Harran all these years, sends greetings. He has returned with his family, servants, cattle, donkeys, and sheep, and he hopes that you will receive him.'"

The men soon returned with such adverse news that Jacob was petrified.

'We met Esau', they said, 'and gave him your message. He is, however, coming to meet you with 400 armed men.'

As there was no time to waste, Jacob divided the people who were with him into two groups. He thought, *If Esau attacks the first group, the other group can escape.* Afterwards, he prayed in anguish, 'O God of Abraham and Isaac, You were the one who instructed me: "Get out of Harran and return to your birthplace, and I will treat you well." I don't deserve any of the mercies and love You have shown to me, for when I left to go to Harran, all I had was my staff, and now I have become two companies. Please save me from my brother Esau. You promised to make my descendants like sands of the sea, too many to count! How can that be if Esau kills us all?'

That night he prepared a present for his brother from his possessions: 200 female goats, 20 male goats, 200 ewes and 20 rams, 30 nursing camels with their young, 40 cows and 10 bulls, 20 female donkeys and 10 male donkeys.

He put a servant in charge of each lot and said to them, 'You go ahead and keep a good distance between each herd. When you meet Esau and he questions you, say to him: "Your servant Jacob sent us ahead with this gift for you, he is also on his way."'

Jacob thought that perhaps the gifts would give him a soft landing with his brother. He then helped his two wives, concubines, and children to cross a ford called Jabbok, along with all his possessions, but he stayed back by himself to continue in prayer.

The fear of being hanged helped his mind to focus. Although Jacob was at his wit's end, he played back in his mind the events of that day many years ago when he had robbed Esau of his rightful inheritance. He recognised that he had been on the run ever since. Esau was his nemesis and vilification for the sins of his past. He involuntarily cried out for deliverance from this man who had become too strong for him.

But before God would help him, there was the matter of Jacob's ways and the duplicity of his character. So an angel came and wrestled with him, seeking to break him. At the defining moment of life, every man or woman who is impudent, presumptuous, self-gratifying, or outright wayward wrestles with their maker. To surrender is to win and be free of the hamstring of rebellion.

That early morning, Jacob won his fight by renouncing his wilfulness and obstinacy and yielding to God's providence for his life. The struggle, however, left him limping as the socket of his hip came out of the joint. A scuffle could result in injuries, leaving scars even after the wounds heal! For a man who had become accustomed to life on the run, being thus disabled posed a serious threat to his survival instincts; he therefore held on to the angel for dear life.

'I will not let you go unless you bless me,' he pleaded, tears streaming down his wizened face.

The angel understood his plight and, wanting to help, asked him, 'What is your name?'

'Jacob, sir, meaning "cheat",' he replied shamefacedly.

The angel reassured him, 'From now on, you will no longer be called Jacob but Israel, for you've wrestled with God and won.' Then the angel blessed him there. Jacob marvelled that he had survived such an awesome ordeal with the angel. It was akin to a face-to-face encounter with God, yet he lived to tell the story.

The turning point in Jacob's life is aptly reflected in the Bible verse that followed this extraordinary encounter between God and man:

> The sun rose above him as he passed Peniel.
> (Genesis 32:31) NIV

God had told the sun to shine again, and the shadows which had been cast over Jacob by the setting sun at Bethel on the night he ran away from Esau were lifted.

WHEN A MAN'S WAYS PLEASE GOD

When you are at sea, all waters look the same; that is why you need a compass. Charting one's way in life can be fraught with pressures—within and without. The way we are wired tends to compromise our value judgement, and we are drawn instinctively to things, people, and situations which are attractive, feel good, or boost our ego. For most people, yielding to good sense in decision-making is an acquired disposition born of experience—many times painful ones when past mistakes cost us dearly. But to choose by sight alone or according to how we feel is oftentimes precarious. Sweet wine can go sour, the man or woman of your dreams today can become the object of your nightmare tomorrow, and the well-watered plains of the Jordan River can become burning fields of brimstone and fire.

God has called us to freedom, but to misuse that freedom will invariably lead to affliction and servitude. You are free to abuse recreational drugs and thereby exchange your freedom for cruel addiction. You are free to make self-serving choices, but you could fall into the hands of the vindictive and vengeful. The list of probable good-versus-bad exchanges is long! If you indulge in sexual impropriety, you risk contacting a wasting disease or being entangled in a soul snare. Your health could fail if you do not treat your body as a fit temple for God's Spirit.

One may be ruined from making poor or uninformed choices or through living without boundaries. However, many have found that a proven way of keeping within safe limits is to live according to God's expectations, illustrated through His Word. Life makes no promises, good or bad, but the Author of Life makes a bold assertion: 'If you come to Me, I will give you rest.' He is waiting patiently. Will you come?

Later on that morning, as Jacob looked up, he saw Esau approaching with an army. Quickly he divided the children among their mothers. He put his concubines and their children in front, Leah and her children next, and Rachel and her son in the rear. Then he himself went ahead and bowed down to the ground seven times as he approached his brother, openly vulnerable.

In bowing to Esau, Jacob was disavowing the blessing which he had fraudulently obtained from their father twenty years earlier when Isaac had pronounced, 'May peoples serve you and nations honour you. You will master your brothers, and your mother's sons will honour you.'

Through this self-abasement, he was willingly laying down the position of the firstborn son which he had stolen from Esau. This was Jacob's restitution to a brother he had offended and whose anger shut him out like iron bars. Jacob was indeed a changed man, and his lust to be first place had dissipated like a vapour.

When a man's ways please God, He makes even his enemies to be at peace with him. Jacob pleased God, and He softened Esau's heart towards him. Instead of attacking Jacob, Esau ran to meet his brother. He fell on him, kissed him, and they wept together.

Then Esau asked, 'Who are these people with you?'

Jacob made all his company to come before Esau, and they all bowed to him.

'They are the wives and children God has given to your servant,' he said.

'And what about all the flocks and herds I met?' Esau probed further.

'I sent them ahead as a gift to you that I may find your favour,' Jacob replied.

'You didn't have to do that. I already have plenty, brother. Keep what you have for yourself.'

But Jacob insisted that Esau should have the gifts if only to show that they were cool and that things were now okay between them, so he accepted them.

That day, God turned what would have been a bloodbath on Mount Gilead into a happy reunion of long-lost brothers. Esau offered to stay on with Jacob through the rest of the journey home. He also invited him to Seir, where he lived, but Jacob asked Esau to go ahead while he made his way slowly because of the children and the nursing animals.

After Esau left, however, Jacob went to a place called Succoth, east of the Jordan, and camped there temporarily. He eventually went on to Shechem in Canaan, where he bought a piece of land and pitched his tent. Once again, as was his custom, he set up an altar there and dedicated it to El Elohe Israel; saying — Mighty is the God of Israel.